COUNT YOUR BLESSINGS

A FAMILY CIRCUS COLLECTION

By
Bil Keane

"The Family Circus," distributed by King Features Syndicate, Inc.

Library of Congress Cataloging-in-Publication Data
Keane, Bil, 1922-
    [Family circus. Selections]
    Family circus—count your blessings / Bil Keane.
       p. cm.
    ISBN 1-56179-366-3
    1. American wit and humor, Pictorial.   I. Title.
NC 1429.K29A4   1995
741.5'973—dc20

95-5724
CIP

Published by Focus on the Family Publishing, Colorado Springs, Colorado 80995
Distributed by Word Books, Dallas, Texas.

Cover Illustration: Bil Keane
Cover Design: Candi L. Park

Printed in the United States of America.

95 96 97 98 99 / 10 9 8 7 6 5 4 3 2 1

Introduction

With small children in a home, it should be easy to COUNT YOUR BLESSINGS—if they'd only sit still while you count! For 35 years my cartoons have shown the fun, tears, laughter, and love in a typical family.

Much in evidence is God's place in the home. While I do not pretend to be an evangelist or preacher, my "inspirational" drawings are often called educational in portraying religion as a natural part of everyday life.

Favorable reader reaction to this material has made me want to assemble this book of "Family Circus" cartoons that focus on the family in a special way.

Not every scene depicts Billy, Dolly, Jeffy, or PJ at prayer, in church, or referring to their Heavenly Father, the angels, or the saints. I believe, however, that any cartoon showing tender love among siblings and parents, or the innocence of children, belongs in this collection.

Here you will find depicted in many ways what, in my estimation, is the strongest, largest, and most blessed congregational gathering in the world: The Family.

Bil Keane

" . . . For all these things we thank you, God."

"God said, 'You're welcome.'"

"There are only seven days in a year. They just keep usin' them over and over."

4

5

"God put topping on everything."

"Mommy, why does 'in a minute' take so long?"

" . . . and each snowflake is different from any other one. It has six sides and a design of its very own."

"It's their anniversity, that's why."

8

"You're wrong. I just have a slight case of the flu. I am NOT dying of old age."

"So far I've got, 'Dear Grandma. I'm fine. How are you?' . . . What else is there to say?"

"Don't stop, Daddy. Sometimes my ears stay up later than my eyes."

"After you die, God plays back all your sins on videotape."

"PJ's lucky. He's just the size of a hug."

"The first commandment was when Eve said, 'Adam, eat that apple.'"

"Are you home, God?"

"I'll never understand grown-ups if I live to be eight."

13

"Why did you put your first and last name on this card for Mommy and Daddy? They know Dolly who."

"I don't like winter 'cause there's never any daytime left over after dinner."

"I want to make this heart full of love,
but I don't know how to draw it."

"Could we have just one more piece,
please, Mommy? We'll eat every
bit of our dinner. WE PROMISE!"

16

"What I don't like is when he gets up in his balcony and talks so long."

"When I grow up, I wanna be a vegetarian!"

"Winter is almost over. The ground's
pokin' up through the snow."

"Do I hafta go to school today?
I feel a little bit absent."

"The things I like to smell best are flowers,
Mommy's perfume, and pastrami."

"I wish they'd have put the extra day
in the summer."

" . . . 'ONE NATION' . . . " " . . .'one nation'. . . "
" . . . 'UNDER GOD'. . . " " . . . 'under God'. . . "
" . . . 'INVISIBLE'. . . " " . . . 'invisible'. . . "

"It's too warm for a sweater. March must be turnin' into a lamb."

22

"You be Honey and I'll be Sweetie."

"The FBI has over 75 million fingerprints."
"So do we."

"Mommy, are we gonna put lights
on our Easter lily?"

"On second thought, don't go to YOUR
room. Go to MY room."

"Did they have Easter yesterday in your town, too, Grandma?"

"Before you come in here, Mommy—you love me, right?"

"If we didn't have rain, there wouldn't
be any grass or flowers or mud."

"All right, what's all this quiet about?"

"My memory isn't as good as my forgettery."

"I'm grounded. I said one more word to my mother."

"I spoiled my appetite with dinner."

"They're all asleep. Now we can finally have some time for ourselves."

"Will you take me to see another
rainbow someday, Mommy?"

"We asked God to bless this yesterday."

"Look, Daddy! Homemade flowers!"

"Just in case you got breakfast in bed, Mommy, how would you want all your eggs cooked!"

"I'll always love you, Mommy. And I'll
always remember your name."

"When clouds get mad, they rain on you."

"I can't wait till I'm in the eighth grade
and know all there is to know."

"God made daddies tall so we can
get things from the top shelf."

"I like dogs 'cause if you're doing something stupid, they don't yell at you.
They do it with you."

"Epistles are the Apostles' wives."

"The phone's ringing, the front doorbell's chiming, the dryer's buzzing, and the oven's dinging!"

"Little kids are cute, aren't they?"

"Is it okay to pray before the test if I don't do it out loud?"

"Mommy, where is my anatomy?"

"Don't worry, Mommy, I didn't walk on your papers."

"Cats are smart. They don't grow too big to fit in a lap."

"Didn't they have colors when you were a little girl, Grandma?"

"Have you decided where he'll go to college?"
"No, we're waiting to see how he'll do in nursery school."

"How much longer till we goeth home?"

"Like it, Daddy? We had to go to three
stores and one ice cream place
before we bought it."

44

"Daddy, what were you before you
were a daddy?"

"Grandma, can we switch to a station
that gets THESE days instead
of THOSE days?"

"The part Daddy likes best about runnin'
three miles is tellin' people about it."

"God put the sky up out of reach so
little kids can't touch it."

"I didn't call for anything in particular, Jill,
just the sound of an adult voice."

"Know what, Daddy?
I love your wife."

49

"Mommy, when you get old, how many grandchildren are you gonna have?"

"You look like we're gonna have a baby-sitter, Mommy."

51

"We went for a ride out where they keep all the scenery."

"You can at least open your eyes, PJ. Eyes can't hear."

"Know what we learned in Bible class?
The Lord is my chauffeur,
I shall not walk."

"Keep up the good work, Daddy, and
maybe you'll get promoted
to 'Mommy.'"

"Aren't you glad I got into the family, Mommy? You don't have to be the only girl."

"I wish roses didn't have thorns."

"I'm glad thorns have roses."

"Mommy, why don't you 'God bless me' when I sneeze 'stead of sayin' 'Cover your mouth'?"

"I think he was expectin' you to be our OTHER grandma."

"Grandma really likes all the drawings we sent her. They're hangin' everywhere!"

"Can I be thankful without eatin' sweet potatoes?"

59

"I'm always 'too little to do things' and 'big enough to know better.'"

"Know what souvenir I wanna take home with me, Grandma? You!"

"No, Dolly, our father art downstairs
watching TV."

"There's one thing from their visit they left
behind that we'll NEVER send back
—memories."

"How do angels get their nightshirts on over their wings?"

"Of COURSE I'd like to be the ideal mother. But I'm too busy raising children."

"The only good thing about goin'
to bed is you're a day closer to
your birthday!"

"I think that might be God's fingernail."

63

"Mommy, are Barfy and Sam the same religion as we are?"

"Y'know that big window at the church with the color pictures on it? . . . "

"We do NOT put play money in the collection basket."

"For the last time, shut that thing off and let's go sight-seeing!"

"Why didn't you go before we got on?"

"Which one should I go for—being
an angel or a saint?"

"How come they're always asleep when
we pass something interesting?"

"Why does Mommy hafta be alone
to medicate?"

"That's gonna be a hard act to follow."

"Do you think butterflies are the little children of angels?"

"I'm tired of Billy bein' the oldest. Why couldn't God have done ME first?"

"Daddy invented a NEW way of doing math: thinking."

"Can I ask God to bless Daddy even
though he's out of town?"

"I love beaches 'cause there's always
an ocean near them."

"I always bring some toys with me
in case I get boring."

"Every day God lets some of the water out
so there's room to play on the beach."

"If I ever get to be an angel, I'd rather play a guitar."

"I think we're in trouble. Mommy just called for William and Jeffrey."

"YOU may think of this as the nuclear age,
but to me it's the paper towel age."

"Have you been a good girl today?"

"Yes, and I'm tired out from it."

"Go ahead, ask her. My mom can tell ya exactly how many days till school starts without even lookin' at a calendar."

"Can I get in on this?"

"When Daddy's in the middle of a good story, a commercial comes over the telephone."

"If the Grinch stole Labor Day, maybe school couldn't open."

"I don't WANT to be your little man.
I just want to be a little boy and
go out and play."

"Daddy, when are we goin' over to the
confession stand?"

80

"When me and PJ are old enough to go to school, who's gonna stay home and take care of you?"

"I said 'maybe' and that's final!"

"That's not a REAL sitter. It's our grandma. She LIKES to take care of us."

"Now that I stopped sucking my thumb, I only have a couple more things to learn to be a teenager!"

"Kindergarten is always the same thing:
sharing, sharing, sharing . . . "

"But, Daddy! Horses don't run
out of gas!"

"When I say my prayers, my fingers hug each other."

"Mommy, did you know that Christopher Columbus invented America?"

"Mommy, will you come look for my blue sweatshirt? You're a better finder than Daddy."

"If Grandma is in her twilight years, you must be at daybreak."

"If you can't get along with your brother and sister, how can you ever expect to get along with the world?"

"Father Forrest said people are made out of dust. Who are we putting together up here?"

"Well, I guess it's up and let 'em at me."

"Dolly's not old enough to have her
woman's intuition yet, is she, Mommy?"

93

"PJ, I love you from the bottom of my heart.
Mommy and Daddy are in the top part."

"Look in this, Daddy, and you'll
see church windows."

"Mommy! The pot's losing its temper."

"They're not trying on clothes.
They're voting."

"Can we 'God bless' dogs, too,
or just people?"

"Did you ever have any little childrens of
your own, Grandma?"

"Billy just said a bad word. Do you wanna hear what it was?"

"Girls are called the opposite sex 'cause they always want to do the opposite of what we want to do."

"All the trees are leavesdropping!"

"I figured out a system for getting along with my mom. She tells me what to do and I do it."

103

"Mommy says dinner will be ready
in 20 minutes if I help her,
10 minutes if I don't."

"I always know when it's Saturday. Daddy
brings his whiskers to breakfast."

"What I like best about church is when the organ makes the whole place shake!"

"You're sayin' grace with your eyes open, Billy! I saw you!"

"If I was Noah, I'd have taken a whole BUNCH of cats instead of just two."

"I think it's just a mild case of unfinished homework."

**"I hear somebody coming.
I'll put you on hold."**

**"Do you think God would mind
if I killed this fly?"**

"The sun's goin' down and pretty soon they'll turn on the moon."

"We learned the fourth commandment: 'Humor thy father and thy mother.' "

"Do we have to start bein' good two weeks before Christmas or three?"

"Does the donkey mean Mary and Joseph were Democrats?"

"Shall I play for you,
pa-rum-pa-pum-pummm. . .?"

"Grandma only likes religious cards, so I'm
sendin' her this one with St. Nick on it."

114

"Billy has to stay in his room. He's been taking after your side of the family again."

"Oh, come let us adore me . . . "

"Get up, Mommy! There's a surprise
all over the neighborhood!"

"I'm in a school play, Mommy. Will you
help me learn my line?"

116

117

"I know what Joseph's first name was—
Saint."

"Wow! Morrie was born on December 24th! He just missed bein' Baby Jesus by that much!"

"Of all living creatures, humans are the only ones who pray."   "Or need to."

119

"Should I lay Mary down in the straw? She's 'specting a baby, y'know."

"Arnold Schwartzman is lucky. Christmas only lasts one day, but Hanukkah lasts eight."

121

"... And there was no room for them at the inn."
"Joseph should've phoned ahead
for a reservation."

"It's very late—I better get in my manger."

"It's what I've been wanting my
WHOLE LIFE!"

"We forgot to put baby Jesus in the
manger on Christmas Eve, Mommy.
He's still in the drawer."

"I got a new sled, but the snow wasn't included."

"Heaven is a great big hug that lasts forever."

"Will we be leaving in a LITTLE while
or a BIG while?"

"Fingers like mittens better 'cause
they don't get lonely in them."

126

"When the children are grown and leave home, we two will be all we have left."

"We two were all we had to start with."

"Why do things that make us happy have to end?"

128